Palates and Palettes
La Romita's Cookbook

Amina Quargnali-Diehl and Alessandro Quargnali-Linsley

ISBN: 0989828808
ISBN-13: 978-0-9898288-0-2

The cover is composed of a background print of olives and leaves and an etching of
Il Convento di La Romita, by Enza Quargnali. Title art by Sharon Zeugin.

ACKNOWLEDGEMENTS...

Palates and Palettes – La Romita's Cookbook would not have been possible without the talents of our La Romita culinary artists. Egizia Bordini and Franca Vincenzoni are responsible, day in and day out, for the fresh, simple, delicious, original food featured at every La Romita meal. We owe a special debt of gratitude to Isaura Betelli, a long-time chef at La Romita who developed most of the recipes featured in previous versions of this cookbook, many of which we still use today. La Romita School founders Enza and Paola Quargnali put together the first spiral-bound-and-photocopied La Romita Cookbook over twenty-five years ago at the urging of countless La Romita participants. A "Thank You" also goes to Enza's son Lars Benson, who produced an updated second edition when the first cookbooks sold out.

We wish to thank the artists who contributed photos of their excellent works – the "Palettes" of the book; Sharon Zeugin, for the title art, and Charlotte Britton, Carol Maddox, Charlotte Attebery, Lisa Guthrie, Fritz Kapraun, Marian Dunn, and Benno Philippson for the samples of their work featured throughout these pages. It is fitting that their art grace these pages as their workshops have graced our school. Thank you, also, to John Sakel for the use of several of his photographs.

Finally, neither this cookbook nor, indeed, La Romita School of Art would have been possible without the thousands of artists and art students who have been coming to La Romita for almost fifty years to paint, teach, eat, laugh, make friends, explore, create and inspire. To all of them: grazie infinite!

... AND THANK YOU

Proceeds from the sale of *Palates and Palettes* will go to support La Romita School of Art, a 501(c)3 not-for profit organization whose mission is to promote cross-cultural understanding and appreciation through the visual and creative arts. The province of Umbria, Italy, has long been a refuge for artists and poets, prophets and saints; through its art workshops, La Romita School immerses artists in the region's cultural richness and diversity and serves as a catalyst for each participant's creative expression and personal growth. La Romita School offered its first summer art workshop in 1966 and gained non-profit status in 1983: as the School approaches its 50th anniversary we thank you for your purchase and your continued support!

La Romita Courtyard – Charlotte Britton

A Tavola alla Romita
At the La Romita Table

Umbria is predominantly hilly or mountainous, and one of the few Italian provinces without a coastline. It is also historically a relatively provincial as well as geographically isolated area and these facts are reflected in local gastronomic traditions which rely heavily on fruits of the forest, field, and stream, as well as livestock and crops suited to hilly, infertile terrain. Boar, hare, wild pigeon and trout all feature prominently in "traditional" Umbrian cooking, as do fresh-picked wild asparagus and chicory, lentils, chickpeas and fava beans, and sheep's milk cheeses. Prosciutto, especially from the north-eastern Umbrian town of Norcia, is the pride of the region, and Umbrian olive oil is considered to be some of the best in Italy.

Umbrian cooking uses fresh, simple ingredients in simple preparations. Very few dishes have more than 4 or 5 ingredients, and the cooking involves simple techniques such as braising and roasting. In fact this can be a problem in translating these dishes for use outside of Italy, as you often can't "fix" a defective or low quality ingredient through kitchen trickery.

The cooking at La Romita is, as you will read in these pages, quintessentially Umbrian in its focus. Take the time to buy high-quality, fresh, local ingredients (especially the olive oil!), resist the temptation to over-season and generally over-do things in your preparation, and you will not be disappointed. La Romita prepares its delicious, healthy meals in a simple kitchen, with simple stainless steel pots and implements. If you've got the best All-Clad gadgetry from Williams Sonoma, etc. by all means use it, but it isn't necessary. Instead, put your energy in sourcing the best pasta, fresh vegetables, cheese, eggs and meat.

The wines served at La Romita are Trebbiano (white) and Montepulciano D'Abruzzo (red). Trebbiano is the grape used to make the well-known DOC "Orvieto" white wine. The Montepulciano D'Abruzzo style is, as the name suggests, not from Umbria but from its neighbor to the southwest, the region of Abruzzo. Montepulciano d'Abruzzo was designated as a DOC, in 1968. It covers most of Abruzzo ranging from Molise in the south, the Marche in the north and inland against the Apennines Mountains. These wines must be at least 85% Montepulciano grapes, with Sangiovese grapes permitted, but not required. We've found that the Montepulciano stands up to Terni's hot summer weather better than the other reds we've tried, although Umbria makes and bottles some excellent red wines based on the Sagrantino grape, two of which have recently received DOCG status (Montefalco Sagrantino and Torgiano Rosso Riserva).

With wine, as with our cooking, we are always innovating and experimenting, bringing you the best and most authentic experience possible. We hope that this cookbook will help you re-create a La Romita moment at home, with that most important ingredient of the Italian table- family and friends. Buon Appetito!

-Amina and Alessandro

Antipasti

Appetizers and Pizza

A tavola non si invecchia.

(One does not age at the table.)

Bruschetta al Pomodoro

[broo.SKEHT.tah ahl poh.moh.DOH.roh] ❖ Bruschetta with Tomato

Ingredients

2 medium tomatoes
1-2 cloves of garlic
2 tsp extra virgin olive oil

1 large leaf of fresh basil or fresh oregano
Sea salt and ground black pepper, to taste
2-3 slices of hearty bread, lightly toasted

Directions

Chop the tomatoes into at least a ¼ inch dice and put in a non-reactive bowl. Mince the basil and/or oregano and add to the tomatoes along with the olive oil. Add a pinch or two of sea salt, stir to combine, and let the mixture stand for 5-10 minutes while you slice and toast your bread. This time gives the salt a chance to draw out the juices from the tomatoes, which mix with the oil to form an elixir that flavors the bread. Once the bread has toasted and cooled slightly, rub each slice with the garlic clove. The hard bread acts a bit like a cheese grater and the heat breaks down the harshness of the garlic.

Spoon the topping onto the bread and serve as an appetizer or part of a light lunch.

Aside from a mixed plate of salumi and bread, there is no more fundamental antipasto that the classic bruschetta al pomodoro. This simple mixture of tomatoes, garlic, salt and olive oil exemplifies the foundation of Italian cooking: quality ingredients, simply prepared to show off their best flavor. Needless to say, use the best tomatoes, olive oil, garlic, and bread available!

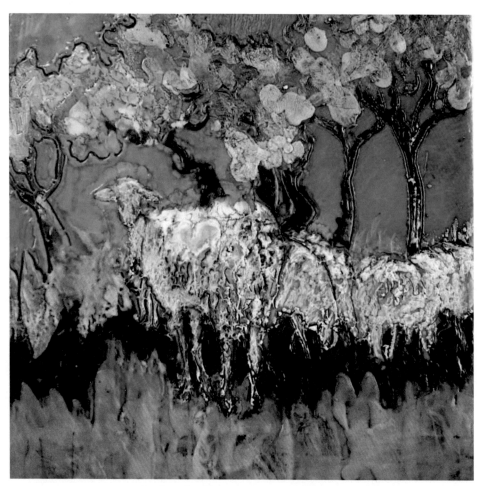

La Romita Sheep – Marion Dunn

Crostini Con Mozzarella e Funghi

[kroh-STEE-nee kohn mohts-sah-REHL-lah eh FOON-gee] ❖ Toasts with Mozzarella and Mushrooms

Ingredients

1 small loaf of crusty white bread
6-8 oz fresh mozzarella cheese, thinly sliced
8 oz mushrooms, roughly chopped
1 clove garlic, crushed and roughly chopped

⅓ c. extra virgin olive oil (approx.)
Sea salt and ground black pepper, to taste
White wine, as needed

Directions

Slice the loaf into approximately ⅜ inch slices. Turn on the oven broiler to low. Place the bread slices on a baking sheet and toast one side for a few minutes, until a bit crunchy or very slightly colored, 3-5 minutes. Remove and cool slightly.

Meanwhile, heat 2 tablespoons olive oil in a medium sized non-stick skillet. Add the chopped mushrooms and the garlic, a large pinch of salt and some black pepper. Cook over medium heat for approximately 5 minutes, adding a small amount of white wine (or water) if necessary, until the mushrooms are uniformly colored and there is still a bit of liquid in the pan. Finely chop the mushroom mixture in a food processor.

Turn the bread pieces over and lightly brush each piece with most of the remaining olive oil. Spread 1-2 teaspoons of the mushroom mixture on each slice. Top with thin slices of mozzarella. Place under a broiler and cook, either high or low, until the cheese has melted, being careful not to burn the bread. Drizzle any remaining olive oil over the *crostini*, and serve warm or at room temperature.

An antipasto served often at La Romita, this is traditionally made with the local bread, which is distinctive for being baked without salt and has a thick, slightly leathery crust and a dense, chewy crumb. Substitute any crusty white bread, but one with a dense crumb and few air pockets works best. Use fresh mozzarella cheese, the kind that comes packed in water. At La Romita, Egizia and Franca use a combination of white button and fresh porcini mushrooms, but use any fresh mushrooms readily available.

A Street in Stroncone- Charlotte Britton

Crostini Rustici

[kroh.STEE.nee ROOS.tee.chee]   ❖   Toasts with Paté

Ingredients

6-8 slices of crusty bread, thinly sliced
12 oz chicken or duck livers
2½ oz prosciutto, finely chopped
½ yellow onion, finely chopped
1 Tbsp non-pareil capers, drained

5-6 fresh whole sage leaves
Juice from ½ lemon
Extra virgin olive oil
Sea salt and pepper
White wine, as needed

Directions

Clean the livers of any fibrous tissue, wash, and pat dry. Using a very sharp knife, gently dice into ½ inch pieces. Using a small sauce or sauté pan, cook the onion with 1 Tbsp of olive oil and the sage leaves over low heat until the onion become translucent, 5-8 minutes. Add the liver and continue to cook until the liver is completely cooked, adding salt and pepper, to taste, 10 minutes. Remove from the heat and allow to cool slightly, approximately 10 minutes.

Remove the sage leaves. Puree the cooked liver in a food processor with the prosciutto and capers. Return to the saucepan and cook over low heat for an additional 10-15 minutes, adding the lemon juice and, if necessary, a bit of white wine to keep the mixture moist: it should have the consistency of very thick salsa or fresh peanut butter. Correct again for salt and pepper. Remove from heat and allow to cool.

Meanwhile, lightly toast both sides of the bread in the oven under a broiler. Brush with a bit of olive oil; spread lightly with the liver pate. Serve at room temperature.

Although not often served at La Romita (for many Americans liver is an acquired taste!) this homemade paté e' is eaten throughout Umbria. The anchovies, lemon, and capers balance the inherent gaminess of the liver: unlike French paté, it has no added saturated fat (just olive oil) so it is both lighter and less creamy. Its flavor improves if kept a day or so in the refrigerator prior to serving.

Slices of this frittata are frequently found served as part of an "antipasto misto" when asparagus are in season. However, frittatas are incredibly adaptable and can be made with any number of vegetables or other fillers. The original La Romita cookbook featured "Frittata di Zucchine", which substitutes 2 small zucchini, sliced into ⅛ inch rounds, for the asparagus.

*The three critical elements to create a good frittata are: a **non-stick pan**, **low heat**, and a (non-stick safe) **spatula**. The pan lets you cook the frittata without much oil, the low heat cooks the eggs through without burning, and the spatula is used to lift the edge as it cooks to allow the uncooked egg to flow underneath.*

Frittata agli Asparagi

[freet.TAH.tah AHL.yee ah.SPAH.rah.jee] ❖ Frittata with Asparagus

Ingredients

1 bunch of asparagus - preferably thin
7-8 large eggs
1 small onion, finely chopped
2-3 Tbsp grated Parmigiano cheese

1 Tbsp extra virgin olive oil
1 tsp sea salt
Freshly ground black pepper, to taste

Special equipment:

10" non-stick skillet (adjust the recipe for larger or smaller pans by adding or removing eggs), silicone spatula

Directions

To prepare the asparagus, remove and discard the bottom ¼ of the stalks and cut into into 2-3 inch batons. Boil them in lightly salted water until mostly cooked, but still a little crunchy, 5-10 minutes depending on thickness.

Set the skillet over medium-low heat while you prepare the egg mixture. In a bowl, beat together the eggs, onion, cheese, pepper, and salt until thoroughly combined - one consistency and color. Stir in the asparagus. Add the oil to the pan, wait a few seconds, and then pour in the egg mixture. For the first few minutes of cooking, periodically lift the edge of the frittata with a rubber spatula to allow egg mixture to reach all parts of the pan.

Once the frittata is mostly cooked and a quick peek to the underside shows a nice brown crust, turn the frittata over. The usual method for doing is to place a plate or rimless cookie sheet on top of the pan, flip them both over, and then slide the frittata back (uncooked-side down) into the pan.

Alternately, if your pan is oven-proof you can slide it under a broiler for a few minutes until the top is brown and crusty.

Pizza di Pasqua al Formaggio

[PEET.tsah dee PAHS.kwah ahl fohr.MAJ.jee.oh] ❖ Easter Cheese Bread

Ingredients

¾ c. freshly grated Pecorino Romano cheese
1 ¼ c. unbleached all-purpose flour
1 tsp baking soda
1 ½ tsp baking powder
½ tsp each, sea salt and ground black pepper

2 eggs
2 Tbsp extra virgin olive oil
½ cup (scant) lowfat or whole milk
1 quart circular Pyrex container*

Directions

Pre-heat an oven to 375 degrees Farenheit. Thoroughly grease the baking dish with vegetable shortening or lard. Sift together the dry ingredients - including the grated *Pecorino* - into a medium mixing bowl. Make a large indentation in the dry ingredients and add the eggs, olive oil, and milk. Mix together thoroughly but do not overstir: the mixture will be quite sticky, like a biscuit recipe or gooey cookie dough. Transfer in large spoonfuls to the baking dish and bake, uncovered, for 35-40 minutes until a toothpick or wooden skewer inserted comes out dry. Allow to cool slightly before removing from the baking dish.

The flavor of the Pizza di Formaggio will deepen and improve over the next couple of days. It's delicious served slightly warmed or toasted, with your favorite cheese, salami or prosciutto and a glass of Prosecco.

A circular shape is traditional. We've found that a one-quart size of an oven-proof glass or Pyrex storage container, such the kind that go directly from the refrigerator to the microwave, work well.

> *In many parts of Italy the word "pizza" is also used for various types of quick- and yeast-leavened breads. Traditionally made only at Easter, you can now buy it year-round in Terni and the immediate environs. We often serve it a part of a light lunch at La Romita: it is delicious with cheese, sliced ham, salami, or prosciutto.*

Umbria near Spello – Carol Maddox

Umbria near Spoleto – Carol Maddox

Pizza con Gorgonzola e Pere

[PEET.sah cohn gohr.gohn.ZOH.lah eh PEH.reh]   ❖   Pizza with Gorgonzola and Pears

Ingredients

1 ⅓ cup all purpose flour, plus extra
1 package active dry yeast
¼ cup warm water
¼ cup warm milk

6-8 oz Gorgonzola, cut into small pieces
3- 4 ripe pears (Bosc or D'Anjou)
Extra virgin olive oil
Sea salt

Directions

Mix the milk, water, and yeast together and allow to proof for 10-15 minutes. Sift the flour and salt together in a separate bowl and make a well in the center. Pour the water and yeast mixture into the well, and add 1 tablespoon of olive oil. Gradually incorporate the water with the flour, first with a fork, then with your fingers, to make a soft, somewhat sticky dough. Dust with flour, cover with a towel and let the dough rise for about 2 -3 hours, or until it has doubled in size. You can also leave the dough to rise overnight in a refrigerator.

Pre-heat the oven to 425 degrees Fahrenheit. Quarter and core the pears and slice into thin slivers. Grease a large baking sheet or ceramic baking stone with olive oil and sprinkle with a bit of cornmeal. Roll out the pizza dough as thinly as possible and transfer to the baking sheet. Arrange the pear slices uniformly over the dough, following with the Gorgonzola pieces. Bake for 18-20 minutes, until the crust is a light golden brown. Allow the pizza to rest for at 5-8 minutes before cutting it into pieces: serve warm.

You can use the same basic technique to make another classic pizza served at La Romita—Pizza Margherita, For the topping, make a simple tomato sauce by simmering a 15 oz can of whole peeled tomatoes for 10 minutes with 1 ½ Tbsp extra virgin olive oil and 1 tsp sea salt, using a wooden spoon to cut the tomatoes into chunks (or use an immersion blender/food processor). Prepare the dough as above, this time spreading with tomato sauce and 6-8 oz of fresh mozzarella cheese. Sprinkle with sea salt and bake until the cheese is melted and bubbly and the pizza crust is a light golden brown. Immediately after removing from the oven, top with a few beautiful leaves of basil, and drizzle with olive oil before serving.

Pizza Margherita was named to honor Queen Margherita of Savoy. The colors of the primary toppings invoke the colors of the Italian flag: green basil, white cheese, and red tomatoes.

Castiglione del Lago – Benno Philippson

Crostoni con Fagioli Bianchi

[kroh.STOH.nee cohn fah.JOH.lee bee.AHN.kee] ❖ Toasts with White Beans

Ingredients

6-8 slices of crusty artisan bread
1 14-16 oz can Cannellini beans, drained
½ small yellow onion, finely chopped

1 small carrot, finely grated or minced
Extra virgin olive oil
Sea salt and ground white pepper (optional)

Directions

In an oven or under the broiler, lighty toast the bread on both sides. In a non-stick skillet, heat 2-3 tablespoons of olive oil over a medium low flame for 60 seconds and add the onion. Cook for 3-5 minutes, until the onion has become translucent. Add the finely grated carrot, a pinch of salt, and cook for an additional 5-8 minutes until the carrot has softened, adding small amounts of water or white wine if needed to prevent burning. Drain the cannellini beans thoroughly. Using a blender or food processor, mix together 1½ cups of the beans with the onion/carrot mixture and adjust the salt if needed, adding ground white pepper if desired. Generously drizzle olive oil on each slice of bread and spread thickly with the cannellini mixture. Serve at room temperature.

A distinctive feature of Umbrian cuisine is its salt-free bread. Pane "sciapo" has been eaten since at least the mid 1500s, in a large area of central Italy that includes all of Umbria and the Marches as well most of Tuscany and northern Lazio. Theories for this curious absence abound: a common one is speculation that because salt was so expensive it was reserved for use in curing meats and cheese. The problem with this theory is that cured meats are common throughout Italy, including many areas where salted bread is ubiquitous. Another popular theory is that the "Salt War" of 1540 between Pope Paul III and the Comune of Perugia led to a local tradition of salt-free bread as a symbol of Perugia's rebellion.

A recent paper by scholar Zachary Nowak points out, however, that the many detailed contemporary accounts of the Salt War do not mention eating salt-free bread as a form of rebellion, and that the current area of salt-free bread consumption is much larger than the areas involved in the Salt War. Nowak's research suggests, rather, that by 1540 eating bread without salt was already part of the area's culinary tradition. Whatever its origin, it is without doubt that Umbria's pane sciapo pairs beautifully with the region's strongly flavored cured meats and cheeses.

Primi

First Courses

"La cucina è di per sé scienza. Sta al cuoco farlo divenire arte."

Gualtiero Marchesi

(Cooking is a science. It is for the cook to make it an art.)

Lake Piediluco – Lisa Guthrie

Minestrone

[mee.neh.STROH.neh]

Ingredients

1 bunch of Swiss chard, chopped	16 oz dried beans - white, red, or even garbanzo,
1 c. green beans, cleaned	soaked overnight
2 medium zucchini	2 medium potatoes
2 medium carrots	2 large tomatoes, quartered
1 large rib celery	3 Tbsp extra virgin olive oil
1 medium onion	Sea salt and pepper to taste

Directions

Chop all of the vegetables into approximately ½ inch dice. In a large soup pot, sautee the onions in the olive oil until softened, 5-10 minutes. Add the tomatoes and cook an additional 10 minutes until they've lost their shape. Fish out the tomato skins and discard. Add in the remaining vegetables and enough water to cover the ingredients. Bring just to a boil, then lower the heat as much as possible, cover, and let simmer for 2 hours or so. Check periodically, and add water if the minestrone looks more stew-like than soup-like. At the 1 hour mark, sample and salt to taste. You may use a vegetable buillon cube for added flavor.

Minestrone is frequently served with grated Parmigiano.

The word minestrone comes from the word "minestra" and literally translates as "big soup", an appropriate name for this hearty, almost stew-like dish. Originally minestrone was not made for its own sake, but as a method of using up the remainders and leftover vegetables from other sauces and contorni. As you look through the recipes in this book, it's easy to see how the remainders of the market-day come together in this soup.

Pasta al Sugo

[PAH.stah ahl SOO.goh]   ❖   Pasta with Tomato Sauce

Ingredients

1 lb of dried pasta, such as penne or rigatoni
1 26-28 oz can of whole peeled Roma tomatoes
3 Tbsp extra virgin olive oil

3-4 cloves garlic, peeled and crushed with a knife
Sea salt and black pepper, to taste
Parmigiano, for serving (optional)

Special Equipment

Using a deep skillet, cast-iron pan or even a dutch oven to make tomato sauce is more effective than using a conventional sauce pan: using a pan with a large surface area helps evaporate liquid from the sauce and condenses the flavor much more effectively than a deep pan with a small surface area.

Directions

In a wide sauce-pan or deep skillet, heat up the olive oil. Add the garlic and gently heat for 3-4 minutes until slightly golden but not burnt. Add the canned tomatoes and bring to a simmer, stirring gently. After 5-8 minutes, break up the whole tomatoes into small chunks with a spoon or stiff spatula. Salt to taste. If the sauce is too sour you can correct by carefully adding ⅛ tsp baking soda to neutralize the acidity: this step is usually unnecessary when using imported Italian tomatoes. Continue to cook at a low simmer until the oil separates from the tomato sauce and floats on top, 20 additional minutes.

Spoon the entire quantity over *al dente* pasta that was cooked in a generous amount of generously salted water. This sauce works equally well with short pasta or spaghetti.

Optional: Add 2-3 Tbsp freshly grated Parmigiano. Serve hot and enjoy!

Sugo Al Pomodoro is the quintessential Italian tomato sauce- light, easy, delicious. With a list of only 4 ingredients, its flavor is largely dependent on their quality. We recommend using imported brands of San Marzano tomatoes which feature minimal added ingredients. For a smoother sauce, puree the tomatoes in a blender prior to using them. Transform this recipe by adding fresh basil to the sauce not more than 5 minutes before using it (lengthy cooking destroys basil's delicate flavor).

Pasta alla Carbonara

[PAH.stah ahl.lah kahr.boh.NAH.rah]

Ingredients

1 lb of dried pasta (spaghetti are traditional)
4 eggs
¼ lb pancetta, finely diced
⅓ c. grated Pecorino Romano cheese
1 clove garlic, crushed

2 Tbsp olive oil
2 tsp freshly ground black pepper
1 tsp salt

Directions

Bring a pot of water to boil for the pasta. In a skillet over low heat, fry the pancetta with the garlic in the olive oil until the fat has rendered and the meat is lightly browned, 8-10 minutes. Remove from heat, but do not drain. In a small bowl, thoroughly beat the eggs, cheese, salt, and pepper together. Set aside.

Salt the boiling water, return to a boil and add the dried spaghetti or fettucine. Cook the pasta until almost *al dente*. Reserve a ½ cup of the pasta water and empty the pot into a colander—however, do not, as with a tomato-based sauce, try to remove most or all of the cooking water from the pasta! Instead, return the (slightly) drained pasta to the pot you boiled it in, and immediately add the pancetta (including the rendered fat) and the egg/cheese mixture. Stir vigorously over very low heat until the egg mixture starts to thicken, but don't let the eggs coagulate on the bottom of the pan. If the pasta starts to dry out, add back in some of the reserved pasta water. The cooling pasta will continue to absorb liquid for about 5 minutes. If desired, use an instant read thermometer to verify the pasta has reached 160° Fahrenheit. Serve immediately!

A variant of this dish calls for replacing two of the eggs with 3 Tbsp to ¼ c. heavy cream.

There are many stories about the origin of this dish and its name. The word carbonara is derived from carbonaro, or "charcoal burner" -possibly a reference to the flecks of black pepper in the creamy egg-based sauce. This dish is generally supposed to come from Rome, and showed up on plates during or just after the World War II. The classic preparation uses guanciale, a type of unsmoked Italian bacon made from pork cheeks. A common substitution is pancetta, made from pork belly. In practice, you can use any type of thick bacon or salt pork.

Penne alla Vodka

[PEHN.neh ahl.lah VOHD.kah] ❖ Penne with Vodka Cream Sauce

Ingredients

5-6 oz pancetta, diced
2 cloves garlic, peeled and crushed
1 28 oz can whole peeled Roma tomatoes,
  pureed in a blender (or use pureed tomatoes)
1.5 lb dried penne pasta*
Extra virgin olive oil

⅓ c. Vodka
⅓ c. heavy cream
3-4 Tbsp freshly grated Parmigiano
Salt and black pepper, to taste

Directions

Heat 1-2 Tbsp olive oil and the crushed garlic in a heavy-bottom sauce-pan over low heat until the garlic turns light yellow, 2-3 minutes. The pan should be large enough so that you can later add the cooked and drained pasta to it. Add the diced pancetta and cook over low-medium heat until the fat in the pancetta turns translucent, approximately 5 minutes. Add the pureed tomatoes, stir, and bring to a gentle simmer. Cook uncovered, stirring occasionally, for 20 more minutes, adding salt if necessary and a bit of black pepper, to taste. Discard the garlic. Add the vodka and cook for 2-3 minutes, until the alcohol has evaporated. Mix in the heavy cream and remove from the heat.

Meanwhile, bring a large pot of salted water to boil. Cook the penne pasta until *al dente*, reserve a cup of the pasta water, and drain thoroughly. Add the pasta to the sauce in the pan, stirring to incorporate while simultaneously adding the grated Parmigiano, adding the reserved pasta wateras necessary. Remove from heat and serve immediately.

This rich and satisfying recipe, translated from metric measurements and then modified to use commonly available pre-packaged quantities, yields enough sauce for 1½ lbs of pasta, more than the usual 1 pound package. Fortunately, it freezes well so you consider saving ⅓ of the finished sauce - about 1¼ cup - for another day.

Orvieto and Sunflowers – Charlotte Attebery

Risotto allo Zafferano

[ree.ZOHT.toh ahl.loh dzahf.feh.RAH.noh] ❖ Risotto with Saffron

Ingredients

1 ¾ c. Arborio rice	½ oz saffron
2 oz each shaved/diced Fontina, Parmesan, and Gruyere cheese	½ (approx) tsp salt
	Extra virgin olive oil
1 small onion, very finely chopped	4 c. (approx) vegetable stock

Directions

Heat the vegetable stock to a gentle simmer, cover, and keep warm. In a separate, heavy-bottom sauce-pan, heat 3 Tbsp olive oil over medium heat. When the oil is hot, add the onion and cook, stirring occasionally, until the onion is translucent, 3-5 minutes. Raise the heat to high and add all the rice at once. Cook for 1-2 minutes, stirring vigorously to ensure that each grain of rice is coated in the oil mixture. The rice kernels will turn translucent, revealing an opaque center: "toasting" the rice this way allows it to better absorb the cooking liquid.

Reduce the heat to medium-low. Add the white wine and continue to cook, stirring, until the wine has mostly evaporated. Add the saffron. Add the hot vegetable stock, 1 ladleful (⅓ cup) at a time, stirring constantly: each time the rice starts to look dry, with airholes in a creamy, wet surface, add additional stock. Make sure to taste and correct for salt. After 18-20 minutes, the rice should be close to done. Add additional stock to achieve the desired consistency, which should be that of a very thick clam chowder: remember that the rice will continue to absorb liquid as it cools. Remove from the heat, stir in the grated cheese, and stir vigorously for a minute or two. This step – the *mantecatura,* is important in bringing out the incredible creaminess associated with risotto. Serve promptly.

This recipe is a simplified version of Risotto alla Milanese that also incorporates features of another classic (northern) Italian risotto, Ris an Cagnon (Risotto with Melted Cheese). The classic Risotto alla Milanese is made with home-made beef stock, beef marrow, butter, saffron and Parmesan cheese. The La Romita version keeps the saffron, but uses only olive oil, and adds to the Parmesan two additional semi-soft cheeses for a dish that is still creamy, yet much lighter and showcases saffron's characteristic yellow color and delicate flavor.

Umbrian Hill Town – Benno Philippson

Risotto con Funghi Porcini

[ree.ZOHT.toh cohn FOON.gee pohr.CHEE.nee]   ❖   Risotto with Porcini Mushrooms

Ingredients

1¾ c. Arborio rice
3½ oz dried porcini mushrooms
15 oz can of tomato puree
1 clove garlic, peeled and crushed
Parseley (flat-leaf), ½ c. finely chopped

2½ c. vegetable broth
2 oz grated Pecorino cheese
Extra virgin olive oil
Sea salt and black pepper, to taste

Directions

Soak the dried porcini mushrooms in enough hot water to just cover them, at least 30 minutes. Drain (reserving the water for later use), chop roughly and reserve. Heat 2-3 tablespoons of olive oil in a skillet, add the crushed garlic and heat for 2-3 minutes. When the garlic starts to turn color, remove it and add the drained, chopped mushrooms and minced parsley and cook for only 3-4 more minutes over medium heat. Add the tomato puree and salt and pepper (to taste). Bring to a gentle simmer and cook for 10 more minutes, stirring occasionally.

Meanwhile, combine the water from soaking the porcini with the vegetable broth, and heat to a simmer in a separate pan or container (a microwave works well). Add the rice to the tomato/porcini mixture and coat the grains thoroughly. Begin adding broth to the risotto, one ½ cup at a time, until the rice has absorbed sufficient liquid to be tender-but-firm, between 18 and 20 minutes. Remember to wait until the rice looks almost dry, with airholes in a creamy wet surface, before adding additional stock; stir the risotto slowly yet consistently.

When the rice has reached the tender-but-firm stage, remove from heat add ¼ to ½ cup additional broth and the grated Pecorino cheese, and stir vigorously for a minute or two. Serve immediately.

"Pecorino" refers to hard cheese made from 100% sheep's milk: there are many regional variations. This particular recipe calls for an aged Pecorino di Norcia, milder and less salty than the "Romano" style Pecorino. Italian Pecorino (other than Pecorino Romano) can be hard to find in the U.S., so good substitutes are aged Manchego (sheep's milk cheese from Spain), Parmiggiano, or Grana Padano - Pecorino Romano will overwhelm the delicate mushroom flavor. Similarly, substitute dried shitake mushrooms (or fresh Portabello) if you cannot find the dried porcini variety.

Risotto al Sugo

[ree.ZOHT.toh ahl SOO.goh]   ❖   Risotto with Tomato Sauce

Ingredients

1 ¾ c. Arborio rice
¼ yellow onion, finely chopped
¼ c. celery, and 1 small carrot, finely chopped
4 oz ground beef
2 oz ground pork
½ c. white wine
1 15 oz can whole Roma tomatoes, pureed

2 ½ c. (approx) beef or vegetable broth
Extra virgin olive oil
Salt and pepper, to taste
1 tsp grated lemon peel
3-4 Tbsp freshly grated Parmigiano
Grated nutmeg (tiny amount)

Directions

Heat 2 Tbsp of oil in a large heavy-bottomed sauce-pan, add the chopped onion, and cook over medium heat until the onion becomes translucent, about 5 minutes. Add the chopped celery and carrot and cook for another 5 minutes, stirring the mixture frequently to keep it from burning. Add the ground meats, a large pinch of salt and a bit of freshly ground pepper. Crumble the meat with a fork or wooden spoon and cook, stirring occasionally, until the meat is uniformly browned. Add ½ c. white wine and cook until it has evaporated, approximately 5 minutes. Add the crushed tomatoes, bring to a low boil and reduce the heat, simmering for an additional 10 minutes, adding additional salt if necessary. At this point, the *sugo* can be used to make lasagna, or used as a sauce for dried pasta like rigatoni or fresh pasta like papparedelle or ciriole.

Heat the broth to a simmer in a separate pan or in the microwave. Add the Arborio rice directly to the tomato sauce, making sure to incorporate the rice thoroughly. Simmer on low heat, stirring slowly, adding small amounts of warm broth to the mixture (½ cup at a time) as needed until the rice has absorbed the liquid but is still slightly chewy, 18-20 minutes. The risotto will have the consistency of a very dense stew or clam chowder. Remove from the heat and add the nutmeg, grated lemon rind, and Parmigiano, and stir vigorously for a minute or two. Serve immediately, on warm plates if possible.

Orecchiette con Cima di Rapa

[oh.rehk.KYEHT.teh kohn CHEE.mah dee RAH.pah]   ❖   "Little Ears" with Greens

Ingredients

1 lb orecchiette pasta
1½ pounds broccoli rabe
2-3 cloves garlic, peeled and crushed
2-3 tsp anchovy paste

Extra virgin olive oil
Pepperonicino Rosso (ground hot pepper)
Salt and pepper, to taste
3-4 Tbsp freshly grated Pecorino Romano cheese

Directions

In a large stock pot, bring water to a boil and salt generously. Prepare the broccoli rabe by cutting off and discarding 4-6 inches of the tough ends, coarsely chopping the remainder into 1½ inch pieces. Wash the rabe, further discarding the larger, coarser stems without any leaves or flower-heads. Add the roughly chopped rabe to the boiling, salted water, bring back to a boil, and cook until the stems are fork-tender, about 8 minutes. Scoop the rabe pieces from the water and place in a colander; keep the water for cooking the pasta.

Press as much water as possible from the rabe pieces. Transfer to a large cutting board and finely chop. Heat 3 tablespoons of oil in a large sautee pan. Add the garlic and cook until lightly colored. Remove the garlic pieces, and add the anchovy paste to the olive oil, mixing to incorporate the paste with the oil. When incorporated, return the garlic to the mixture and add the finely chopped broccoli rabe. *Optional:* add ½ tsp of the hot pepper. Cook over medium low heat for 10 minutes, adding a bit of water or broth if necessary to keep the mixture moist.

Bring the salted water back to a roiling boil, adding more water if necessary, and add the orecchiette pasta. Cook until al dente. Before draining the pasta, remove 1 cup of the starchy, salty water and set aside. Add the cooked, drained pasta to your serving bowl, then add the broccoli rabe mixture and mix thoroughly to incorporate, adding a few tablespoons of the reserved pasta water as necessary. Stir in grated pecorino cheese and serve immediately.

"Cima di Rapa" are turnip greens. At La Romita we use either turnip greens or broccoli rabe, depending on what's in season. For this recipe we use fresh broccoli rabe since that's readily available in many stores across the United States, though you could easily substitute chard or even spinach. Orecchiette pasta - little ears - is the traditional, and best shape, for this dish, although you can of course substitute another short pasta shape such as conchiegle (shells).

Lasagna con Mortadella e Prosciutto Cotto

[lah.ZAH.nyah kohn mohr.tah.DEHL.lah eh proh.SHOOT.toh COHT.toh] ❖
Lasagna with Mortadella and Cooked Ham

Ingredients

⅔-¾ lb flat lasagna sheets*
    (enough to create 5 layers in an 8 by 8 dish)
3-4 oz mortadella
3-4 oz prosciutto cotto**

3-4 oz Fontina cheese
1 ¼ c. heavy cream
⅔ c. freshly grated Parmigiano
Butter (to grease the baking pan)

Directions

Pre-heat an oven to 375 degrees Fahrenheit. Prepare salted, boiling water to cook the lasagna sheets. Using a food processor, mince the mortdella and prosciutto cotto and set aside. Grate or process the Fontina into large crumbs (briefly chilling this semi-soft cheese in the freezer prior to grating helps considerably). Generously butter an 8 by 8 baking dish. Set out a clean, slightly damp cotton or linen dish towel on which you will lay the blanched lasagna sheets.

Briefly cook the lasagna sheets: Using tongs, gently place enough sheets for 2 layers of the lasagna in the boiling water, and remove after 30-60 seconds. If you try to cook all the lasagna at once, the sheets will stick and clump together before you can layer them; if you cook longer than 60 seconds, the pasta may tear. Drain the lasanga sheets on the damp cloth. Layer the bottom of the dish with the lasagna sheets, sparingly sprinkle with one-fifth of the ground mortadella/prosciutto mix, one-fifth of the grated Fontina cheese, and 1-2 tablespoons of grated Parmesan. Drizzle (again, sparingly) with ¼ cup heavy cream. Add another layer of pasta and top with ingredients, as above. Bring the salted water back up to a boil, cook the remaining pasta sheets, and finish assembling until you have five layers of pasta topped with filling and cream.

Bake for 30-40 minutes or until the top layer turns a light golden brown. Cool for 10-15 minutes before cutting and serving. This dish can be assembled and stored in the refrigerator for up to a day before being baked.

In Italy the pasta for lasagna is almost always either made by hand or, as at La Romita, bought fresh and used the same day. Most freshly made lasagna sheets available in the U.S. are thick by Italian standards, but a good choice if available. If not, look for dried lasagna sheets. The plain ones (without the ridged edges) work best.

**A good substitute for prosciutto cotto (cooked ham) is plain, unsmoked, cured ham from the deli, but avoid styles that have "honey" or "maple" in the name.*

Linguine al Pesto

[leen.GWEE.neh ahl PEH.stoh] ❖ Linguini with Pesto

Ingredients

1 lb dried or fresh linguine pasta
2 c. tightly packed fresh basil leaves
1 clove garlic
¼ c. pine nuts

¼ c. extra virgin olive oil
½ tsp sea salt
Pepperoncino or ground black pepper, to taste
½ c. freshly grated Parmigiano cheese*

Directions:

Add all the ingredients except the cheese into a food processor and pulverize until smooth.

Cook the pasta – spaghetti or linguine, dried or fresh – as usual in plenty of well-salted water. Before draining the pasta, reserve 1 cup of the salted, starchy water.

Add the pesto to the linguine and mix, incorporating the grated cheese and adding reserved pasta water if the dish is too dry. Serve!

You can also use a 50/50 mixture of Parmigiano and grated Pecorino Romano, for added bite. A squeeze of lemon juice in the mixture will help keep the pesto bright green. Pesto freezes very well, so long as cheese hasn't been added. To freeze, spoon it into the bottom of a 1 quart freezer bag and squeeze out the extra air. To use, just drop the sealed ziplock in a bowl of warm water for 20 minutes to defrost, and squeeze it out into a bowl and finish the recipe.

The word pesto comes from the Italian word "pestare" by way of the Genovese dialect. Pestare means "to pound", and shares roots with the word "pestle", which makes sense because the traditional way of making pesto involves using a mortar and pestle to combine the ingredients. These days a food processor does the heavy lifting, but if you have a mortar and pestle and are willing to spend a few extra minutes, grinding the nuts and garlic together before adding the leaves has a distinct affect on the texture of the sauce. As always, the best ingredients yield the best flavor. Home grown or organic basil and garlic, a good quality olive oil, and the best imported Parmigiano, Grana Padano, and/or Pecorino you can reasonably afford will be worth the effort in the final dish. Many recipes call for substitutions or additions (such as parsley, etc), but Egizia and Franca stick to this classic recipe.

Secondi

Second Courses

> *"La pasta: se non ci fosse stata, la sarebbero dovuto inventare."*
>
> Anonymous
>
> (Pasta: if it hadn't already existed, it would have had to be invented.)

Ancient Stairway – Marian Dunn

Fagottini di Maiale al Tartufo

[fah.goh.TEE.nee dee mah.YAH.leh ahl tar.TOO.foh] ❖ Truffle-Stuffed Pork

Ingredients

1¼ pounds pork loin, sliced very thinly
10-12 fresh sage leaves
10-12 slices of semi-soft, mild, meltable cheese
    such as Fontina or Emmenthal
⅔ c. bread crumbs (unseasoned)

⅓ c. grated Parmigiano
2-3 oz truffle paste
2 eggs, beaten
Extra virgin olive oil
Salt and pepper, to taste

Directions

Pre-heat the oven to 375 degrees Farenheit. Mix the breadcrumbs and Parmigiano in a shallow baking dish or large plate. Taste and add salt if necessary, and set aside. Lightly coat a large baking sheet with olive oil.

On a large cutting board, assemble the *fagottini* as follows: pork loin slice + thin slice of cheese + thin layer of truffle paste + sage leaf + pork loin slice -- you are making little sandwiches of pork, truffle paste, and cheese. If necessary, use a toothpick to hold the sandwich together, but in making this dish at home we were surprised to find this precaution unecessary. When the *fagottini* are assembled, dip each one in the egg mixture and then coat with the bread-crumbs/Parmigiano mixture: place on the baking sheet. Bake, turning once, for approximately 30 minutes or until a meat thermometer registers 145°*.

Transfer to a plate, garnish with lemon slices, and drizzle a bit of high-quality olive oil for taste. Serve warm, so that the cheese is still melted. Delicious!

In 2011, the USDA lowered the minimum safe cooking temperature for pork to 145° Fahrenheit from 160°.

Fagottino means "little bundle" and in this case the pork slices are combined with cheese, sage, and truffle paste into little bundles and then baked-- delicious! We've given the original ingredients as used at La Romita, but listed appropriate substitutes where appropriate that will yield similar results in terms of taste and texture. At La Romita, we use a fresh, store-bought paste made from minced fresh truffles mixed with other mushrooms: in the U.S., truffle paste can be found online (Amazon) or in many specialty Italian stores.

Pollo al Tartufo

[POH.loh ahl tar.TOO.foh] ❖ Chicken with Truffles

Ingredients

1 2½ to 3 lb chicken
1 15-16 oz can crushed tomatoes
1 c. dry white wine
½ medium onion, finely chopped

1-2 cloves garlic, peeled and minced
1 small black truffle, thinly sliced
Sea salt and pepper, to taste

Directions

Dress the chicken pieces by removing the excess fat and much of the skin. Wash and pat dry, then season well with salt and pepper. Heat 2 Tbsp of oil in a large skillet over medium-high heat and carefully add the chicken, being careful not to crowd the pan. Cook them until lightly browned on both sides (3-4 minutes per side), reduce the heat and cook them until they reach an internal temperature of 160 degrees Fahrenheit (residual heat will take them up to 165°), 15-20 additional minutes. Remove the meat to a warm dish and lightly tent with foil while you make the sauce.

Discard all but 2 Tbsp of the fat from the pan. Return the pan to a medium-low heat, add the garlic and onion, and cook until the onion is translucent. Deglaze the pan with the white wine making sure to scrape up "the brown bits" and reduce well. Add the crushed tomatoes, and simmer for another few minutes.

Return the chicken to the pan and let it soak up a bit of the sauce and come back to temperature. Then transfer the chicken onto a serving dish, cover with thin slices of black truffle, and finally spoon the rest of the sauce over the dish.

Note: Truffle can be both hard to find and expensive in the States. While not the same, some thinly sliced porcini or Portobella mushrooms, well browned in a pan with a little olive oil, is also delicious.

This is another dish highlighting the black truffle, one of Umbria's regional specialties. Truffles are the "fruit" of a fungus that grows on the roots of forest trees, particularly oak and hazelnut. Up the Valnerina (Valley of the Nera River) to the northeast of Terni, three rivers pass through forests of these trees around the town of Norcia and create the perfect environment for tartufi neri. *The best ones are gathered starting in the fall, with the season peak marked by the* Mostra Mercato del Tartufo Nero *truffle festival in February.*

Filetto di Maiale all' Arancio

[fee.LEHT.toh dee mah.YAH.leh ahl ah.RAHN.choh] ❖ Pork Tenderloin with Orange

Ingredients

2 pork tenderloins, approx 2 lbs
2 medium oranges
1-2 tsp green peppercorns
2-3 cloves garlic, roughly chopped.
½ c. white wine

1 6-inch piece of fresh rosemary
Extra virgin olive oil
Sea salt
1 bay leaf (optional)

Directions

Preheat an oven to 400 degrees Fahrenheit. Cut one orange into thin wedges ⅜ to ¼ inch thick, removing the pith from the orange's center. Lay the tenderloins out and make a series of cuts in the meat approximately 1½ inch apart and ½ to ⅔ the thickness of the tenderloin. Place an orange wedge, rind facing out, into each cut in the meat. Season the tenderloins with salt. Drizzle olive oil on the bottom of an oven-proof baking or casserole dish, and arrange the tenderloins so that they do not touch each other.

Sprinkle the tenderloins with the cloves of garlic, the rosemary (cut into smaller pieces) and the green peppercorns. Add a ½ cup of white wine. Cook at 400 degrees for 30-40 minutes, turning the tenderloins over every 10 minutes or so to coat them in the cooking juices, until a meat thermometer inserted into the pork registers 145 degrees*.

Remove from the oven, tent with tin foil, and let sit for 5 minutes. Meanwhile, cut the remaining orange into wedges or slices. Discard the cooked orange. Slice the meat, arrange on a serving platter, garnish with the fresh orange slices, and season with the reserved cooking juices. Serve warm.

*In 2011, the USDA revised its recommendation for the minimum cooking temperature for pork down from 160°. Cooking to the lower temperature results in a moister filetto.

This is one of our favorite ways to cook pork at La Romita. The lean pork cooks quickly, and the fresh orange adds a touch of sweetness and acidity that is refreshing in the hot summer months. Although navel oranges will work, they are too sweet for best results. A better choice are Valencia oranges or, for an exotic touch, blood oranges.

Straccetti alla Rucola

[strah.CHEHT.tee ahl.lah ROO.coh.lah] ❖ "Rags" of Beef with Argulua

Ingredients

1 to 1¼ lb thinly sliced beef
4 c. arugula ("rocket")
1 clove garlic
¼ c. (approx.) red or white wine

Extra virgin olive oil
Sea salt and black pepper, to taste
1½ Tbsp balsamic vinegar (optional)
¼ c. freshly shaved Parmigiano

Directions

In a metal skillet (preferably <u>not</u> non-stick), heat 2 tablespoons of olive oil over medium heat, coating the bottom of the pan. Crush the garlic cloves with a back of a knife and add them to the oil until lightly colored, 1-2 minutes. Remove the garlic, increase the heat to high and add the sliced beef. Season the meat with salt and pepper and cook, stirring, until cooked through, about 5 minutes. As the liquid from the meat evaporates, add the red wine by tablespoon, gradually reducing the juices in the pan to approximately 3 tablespoons, 2-3 additional minutes. Set aside to cool slightly. Optional: replace some or all of the wine with balsamic vinegar, for a more complex acidic flavor and darker color.

Meanwhile, roughly chop the arugula into large pieces. Toss with the balsamic vinegar and the remainder of the olive oil, 30 seconds. Gently incorporate the Parmigiano shavings. Arrange the *straccetti* on a serving platter (along with any remaining sauce from the cooking), and top with the arugula and Parmesan mixture. Serve warm.

> *This delicious and visually stunning dish, added to the La Romita menu in the last five or six years, is quickly becoming a participant favorite! In Italy, this dish is made using beef from a cut Italian butchers call the* noce, *also used in many dishes involving thinly sliced cutlets of veal or beef (e.g. veal scaloppini). The closest American equivalent is a cut called "Tip Steak" or "Tip Roast," but a thick sirloin or Tri-tip steak work well. Cut (or have your butcher cut) the meat across the grain in very thin slices – "quasi trasparenti" (almost transparent). Further cut these slices into strips 1 inch by 2-3 inches, so they resemble "little rags," or* straccetti.

San Xavier – Fritz Kapraun

54

Salmone al Gratin

[sahl.MOH.neh ahl GRAH.teen] ❖ Baked Salmon

Ingredients

1 to 1¼ pound salmon steaks*, ¾ inch thick
1 ½ c. plain Italian bread crumbs
1-2 cloves garlic, minced
½ c. fresh Italian parsley, finely chopped

¼ to ⅓ c. freshly squeezed lemon juice
Extra virgin olive oil
Sea salt and black pepper, to taste

Directions

Pre-heat an oven to 350 degrees Fahrenheit. Wash the salmon steaks and pat them dry. In a bowl, combine the bread crumbs, garlic, parsley, and lemon juice together with the ¼ cup olive oil to form a crumbly paste. The bread crumbs should be just moist enough to clump together.

Line a baking tray with parchment paper (or lightly coat a baking tray with olive oil). Lightly season one side of the salmon steaks with salt and pepper and lay them seasoning-side-down on the parchment paper. Coat the other side of the fish with the breadcrumb mixture, firmly pressing the breadcrumbs down and around each piece of fish so that each piece is thoroughly covered. Bake for 20-25 minutes: the breadcrumbs should turn a light golden brown. Remove, cool slightly, garnish with fresh slices of lemon, and serve.

*At La Romita, this dish is often prepared with fresh cod steaks (merluzzo), but salmon appears to be almost universally available.

With its long coastline, it's not surprising that fish features prominently in Italian cuisine. Fish is less common in Umbria, and when found is usually river or lake fish: either trout from Umbria's rivers, or lake fish from lakes Piediluco and Trasimeno, which include pike (luccio), a type of carp (regina), and freshwater eel (anguilla). The most common preparation for the freshwater fish is stuffed with fresh herbs such as parsley and wild fennel and then grilled, almost always over wood coals. Eel is usually stewed. When we serve fish at La Romita, we most often serve the larger ocean fish because they can stand up to baking, and are easier to serve and eat. A fresh trout from the Valnerina or Piediluco is, however, hard to beat!

Basic Béchamel

Melt 1 Tbsp butter in a small saucepan, add 1 Tbsp flour and cook the paste for about a minute until it loses its "floury" smell. Slowly add a cup of warmed milk (the microwave is perfect for this), a pinch of salt and a pinch of nutmeg, stir continuously over low heat until all lumps are gone and the mixture thickens. To make a thicker sauce, double or triple the butter & flour.

Crepes con Prociutto Cotto

[KREPS cohn proh.SHOOT.toh COH.toh]   ❖   Crepes with Cooked Ham

Ingredients

2 eggs
2 Tbsp. salted butter
⅔ c. flour
1 c. + 2 Tbsp reduced fat milk
Sea salt

1 c. (approx) Béchamel sauce (opposite)
4-5 oz thinly sliced cooked ham
5-6 oz fresh mozzarella, diced

Directions

For the crepes: Melt the butter and cool slightly. Thoroughly mix together the butter, egg, and milk, as well as the pinch of salt. Add the flour in small amounts, stirring vigorously to avoid forming clumps. The batter will be very thin and runny. Pre-heat a crepe-pan over a medium-high flame, using a little non-stick spray or butter if necessary, and pour 2-3 tablespoons of batter into the pan to form a very thin layer. When cooked through, turn the crepe to brown the top, about 30 seconds. Set aside and keep warm. Prepare the béchamel sauce.

To assemble the crepes: Preheat an oven to 350 degrees Farenheit, and butter a casserole or baking dish. Place a slice of ham and thin slices of mozzarella cheese onto the crepe and roll it up. Arrange the rolled-up crepes in the baking dish and drizzle with the béchamel sauce. Bake for 20-25 minutes. Serve warm. Optional: after 15 minutes, remove and sprinkle with 2-3 Tbsp of Parmigiano. Raise heat to 375° and return to the oven for an additional 10 minutes. Serve warm.

This recipe, whose likely origin is France by way of Northern Italy, has become a staple of the La Romita table. This recipe makes approximately 10 8-inch savory crepes. Special crepe pans are available on Amazon for less than $25, but you can substitute any 10" non-stick pan or even a griddle. Non-stick will result in very pale crepes and for that reason we recommend using one made of steel.

Umbria, near Ferentillo – Carol Maddox

Villa Aspreta, Amelia – Carol Maddox

Spezzatino di Vitella

[speht.sah.TEE.noh dee vee.TEHL.lah] ❖ Veal Stew

Ingredients

1 ½ lb of lean beef such as sirloin
2 cloves garlic, peeled and crushed
4-5 fresh sage leaves
1 Tbsp fresh rosemary
¾ c. white wine

½ c. (3-4 oz) green brined olives, drained
Extra virgin olive oi
Sea salt
1 tsp freshly ground green pepper

Directions

Cut the beef into uniform 1 to 2 inch rectangular chunks and season with salt and pepper. Roughly chop the herbs and set aside. Heat 2-3 tablespoons of olive oil in a dutch oven or deep, wide-bottomed skillet. When the oil is hot, add the meat pieces and brown, 2-3 minutes per side. Lower the heat to medium, add the crushed garlic and chopped herbs, turn to make sure the herbs and cooking liquid coat the meat, and cover. Continue cooking for an additional 5-10 minutes. Add the wine and green olives and continue to cook uncovered for 10-15 more minutes, allowing the liquid to mostly evaporate. Taste and add salt as necessary. Remove a piece of meat to check for doneness; continue to cook a few minutes longer if necessary, adding either additional wine or water as needed (there should be a few tablespoons of flavorful cooking liquid left). Your total cooking time for this dish should be about 30 minutes. Remove and drizzle generously with olive oil before serving; garnish with lemon wedges or slices.

Beef and veal are quite expensive in Italy and the cuts of meat that require long cooking times to become tender (for example, osso bucco, which is high in fat and connective tissue) are rarely used in local cooking. "Spezzatino di Vitella" in fact calls for chunks of yearling veal – "vitellone" – which come from a yearling-or-so animal rather than a very young calf. Because the cooking time for this dish is short - it's essentially a quick braise - there is no time to break down the collagen found in brisket or other types of beef that are suited for long cooking. Avoid pre-packaged "stew" meat. Instead, look for sirloin, rib-eye roast, or top loin steak, and cut it yourself into chunks or have it prepared by a butcher.

Contorni

Side Dishes

> *"Ci sono tante cose importanti nella vita, la prima è mangiare, le altre non conosco."*
>
> Anonymous
>
> (There are many important things in life. The most is to eat well, and I don't know the rest.)

Field Patterns – Lisa Guthrie

Verdure al Peperoncino

[vehr.DOO.reh ahl peh.peh.rohn.CHEE.noh] ❖ Greens with Red Pepper

Ingredients

2 bunches (approx 1 lb each) chard or chicory
1 clove garlic, peeled and crushed
2 Tbsp extra virgin olive oil, plus a bit extra

Sea salt and freshly ground pepper, to taste
A small amount of *peperoncino* (ground red pepper)
(optional)

Directions

To prepare the chard, remove and discard the stalks level with the leaf. Cut each broad leaf in half along the vein, and then cut each half into large pieces, approximately two inches by two inches. Wash the pieces thoroughly in cold fresh water and drain. Place the chard in a stockpot or dutch oven along with ½ cup of water (enough to keep the leaves from sticking to the pot). Cook over medium-high heat for 8-10 minutes or until the chard is wilted and has lost about half of its volume. Drain the chard in a colander, pressing with the back of a wooden spoon or spatula to squeeze out as much water as possible.

Transfer the chard to a cutting board and chop coarsely. Heat the olive oil and garlic gently in the bottom of the discarded stockpot/sauce-pan, until the garlic is just slightly colored, being careful not to burn - 2-3 minutes. Return the drained and chopped chard to the pan and coat thoroughly with the olive oil. Season to taste with salt and, if desired, peperoncino, and let cook on a very low heat for 10 to 15 more minutes, uncovered. This allows the flavor to develop and additional water to evaporate.

This dish can be made ahead of time and stored in the refrigerator, which will allow the flavors to develop further. Discard the garlic prior to eating or storing.

In Italy, many dark green leafy vegetables – for example chard, spinach, and chicory – are prepared in this fashion, especially in the winter. Most Umbrian grocery stores sell balls of pre-cooked leafy greens in their deli sections, ready to be taken home for additional seasoning as described above. Traditionally, when prepared at home, the pre-cooked leaves are allowed to cool and squeezed by hand to remove excess moisture, then stored for up to 3 days in the refrigerator.

Fagiolini al Pomodoro

[fah.joh.LEE.nee ahl poh.moh.DOH.roh] ❖ Green Beans with Tomatoes

Ingredients

½ lb green beans, washed and trimmed
8 oz crushed canned tomatoes
¾ c. water
1-2 cloves garlic, crushed

1 Tbsp extra virgin olive oil
Fresh basil, marjoram, or oregano
Sea salt and freshly ground black pepper

Directions

In a medium, wide-body sauté pan, saute the garlic in the olive oil over medium-low heat until the garlic is lightly colored, 3-4 minutes. Add the crushed tomatoes. Season with salt, and add the water ¼ cup at a time. The amount you add will depend on the consistency of the tomatoes, which should remain fairly chunky. Bring to a simmer, add the green beans, and simmer in the tomato sauce. Add additional water if necessary until just past al dente, about 20 minutes. When you believe you have approximately 5 minutes of cooking time left, season with a few twists of freshly ground black pepper and, if desired, a small amount of chopped fresh basil, marjoram, or oregano. Serve warm.

Green beans have a nice long season, and are a delicious accompaniment to a summer meal. Fagiolini al Pomodoro is a common preparation in Umbria (and Tuscany): essentially a short braise of the bean in a basic tomato sauce. As always, start with the best, freshest ingredients available to you.

Valle di San Martino – Fritz Kapraun

Zucchine Trifolate

[dzook.KEE.neh tree.foh.LAH.teh]   ❖   Sauteed Zucchini

Ingredients

2 medium zucchini
1 large clove of garlic, lightly crushed
2-3 Tbsp extra virgin olive oil

Sea salt and freshly ground black pepper
Fresh marjoram or basil (optional)

Directions

Select zucchini that are not too large, no more than 1 inch in diameter, smooth and firm throughout. Quarter the zucchini lengthwise, then cut each quarter into ⅛ inch slices, so that you have uniform wedges. Heat the olive oil over medium heat in a 12 inch skillet. Add the garlic and cook until slightly colored, 2-3 minutes. Remove and discard. Add the zucchini to the pan, distributing uniformly in a single layer. Sprinkle with salt and pepper and cook for 2-3 minutes: the side in contact with the oil should be a light golden brown. Using a large spoon or spatula, stir the zucchini to brown the other side, again 2-3 minutes. Stir again, partially cover and cook for an additional 5 minutes. At this time, you can add a small amount of fresh or dried marjoram or basil. The zucchini are done when they are soft, but not mushy or translucent. Remove from the heat and immediately transfer to a serving dish to prevent the zucchini from continuing to cook in the residual heat of the pan. Serve immediately!

This simple preparation brings out the sweetness of the vegetable, and the cooking technique lends itself to other types of squash. Keeping the pan hot and (mostly) uncovered keeps the zucchini from becoming mushy. Try using the same technique with similar sized pieces of eggplant or red bell pepper—if you mix all three vegetables, you get another Italian classic called "Bandiera Italiana," for the way the colors of the dish recall the Italian flag.

Umbrian Hill Town – Charlotte Attebery

Finocchio al Forno

[fee.NOH.kyoh ahl FOHR.noh]   ❖   Baked Fennel

Ingredients

5-6 fennel bulbs⁺, cleaned and sectioned vertically,
  like an orange
¼ c. plus 2 tsp freshly grated Parmigiano

¾ - 1 c. Béchamel (to taste)
Extra virgin olive oil
Sea salt and freshly grated white pepper

Directions

Prepare the béchamel according to the directions on p. 48, using the following proportions: 1 ½ c. milk, 3 Tbsp butter, 2 Tbsp flour, a pinch of salt, and a tiny amount of fresh nutmeg.

Preheat the oven to 400 degrees Fahrenheit. Bring a pot of lightly salted water to a rolling boil and add the fennel segments. Cook until slightly tender, between 6-8 minutes. When the fennel is partially cooked, arrange the segments evenly in a buttered 9 x 9 baking dish. Season with white pepper. Sprinkle generously with Parmigiano, then drizzle with ¾ c. to 1 c. béchamel, depending on personal preference. Bake until the béchamel and cheese start to color slightly, approximately 20 minutes. Season to taste with freshly grated pepper and serve.

* When selecting fennel, the bulb should be firm, smooth, and heavy for its size (this indicates freshness, as the bulb has not lost water to storage and dehydration). To clean and trim a fennel bulb: cut the fleshy leafy stalks completely off at the top of the bulb. Cut a slice off the bottom of the bulb and discard the outermost segments, which are the toughest and usually bruised and/or discolored.

There are certain flavors that are far more common in Italy than in the United States, and one of these anise or licorice. Anise seed is used to flavor liquors and sweets throughout Italy: in Umbria you can find slightly sweet, rock-hard doughnut-shaped cookies called "ciambelle all'anice" in any grocery store, as well as a number of after-dinner alcoholic digestive that are both bitter and licoricey. Artichokes, with their slight licorice taste, are used extensively in Umbrian and Roman. This recipe highlights fennel bulb, another vegetable known for its slight anise flavor.

Pomodori Aglio e Maggiorana

[poh.moh.DOH.ree AHL.yoh eh mahj.joh.RAH.nah] ❖

Tomatoes with Garlic and Marjoram

Ingredients

4-6 large, ripe heirloom tomatoes
2-3 garlic cloves, peeled and sliced thin
½ c. crushed or pureed tomatoes

1 Tbsp fresh marjoram, finely chopped
Extra virgin olive oil
Sea salt and freshly ground black pepper

Directions

Preheat an oven to 400 degrees Farenheit. Cut the tomatoes in half horizontally. Drizzle 1-2 Tbsp olive oil on the bottom of a glass baking dish or casserole pan. Thin the crushed/pureed tomatoes with 1/4c water and pour into the dish. Arrange the tomato halves, cut-side up, in the puree and sprinkle the tops with the garlic and fresh marjoram. Spoon an additional 2 Tbsp of olive oil over the tops of the tomatoes. Salt generously and add black pepper, to taste. Cover the dish with aluminum foil and bake for 30 minutes, then remove the foil and bake another 20-30 minutes until the tomatoes are soft all the way through. Remove from the pan and drizzle with the cooking juices and a bit of fresh olive oil. Serve warm.

This dish can also be prepared a day ahead and re-heated briefly in a microwave before serving.

Patate "La Romita"

[pah.TAH.teh lah roh.MEE.tah] ❖ Potatoes "La Romita"

Ingredients

2 pounds thin-skinned potatoes
2-3 cloves garlic, peeled and roughly chopped
A 6-8 inch piece of fresh rosemary

Extra virgin olive oil
Sea salt and black pepper, to taste

Directions

Pre-heat the oven to 450 degrees Farenheit. Peel the potatoes and cut them into uniform, approximately ½ inch cubes. Boil water in a large stockpot and salt generously, as if for pasta. Blanch the cubed potatoes in the boiling water for 2-3 minutes, then drain. Remove the leaves from the rosemary stem and roughly chop. Using the drained stockpot or a large bowl, toss the blanched potatoes with the olive oil, rosemary, garlic, and salt and pepper. Transfer to a large baking tray, adding a bit of additional olive oil if necessary to coat the tray: ideally the sheet should be large enough so that the potatoes are in a single layer. The potatoes will brown better in a metal tray than in a ceramic or glass dish.

Bake at 450° for 40-45 minutes, turning every 15 minutes. Remove and allow to cool for a few minutes before transferring to a serving dish. Drizzle with a little additional olive oil and serve warm

Note: The above is Egizia and Franca's preferred method. In our United States La Romita test kitchens, we often have good results omitting the blanching step in favor of simply soaking the cut potatoes in water to remove excess starch.

At La Romita we use the red-skinned Colfiorito potato whenever available. This Désireè variety of potato is grown in the Colfiorito plateau, northwest of the bustling town of Foligno, straddling the border between hilly Umbria and the more mountainous Marches. The patata rossa di Colfiorito has straw-colored flesh and red skin and is highly prized for making gnocchi (potato dumplings) and chiambelle dolci (donuts). In the U.S., we've found using yellow Yukon potatos works well; stay away from Russet or Idaho varieties.

Dolci, Liquori e Caffe

Desserts, Liquors and Coffee

> *"Buona cucina e buon vino, è il paradiso sulla terra."*
>
> Enrico IV, H.R.E
>
> (Good food and good wine is paradise on Earth.)

Crostata di Marmellata

[croh.STAH.tah dee mahr.meh.LAH.tah] ❖ Jam Tart

Ingredients

2 c. all-purpose, unbleached flour
½ c. sugar
1 tsp salt
1 tsp baking powder

½ c. unsalted butter, cold and cubed
2 eggs, lightly beaten
Zest from 1 lemon
6-8 oz jam, preserves or marmalade

Directions

Sift together the flour, sugar, salt and baking powder. Using a pastry tool or fork, cut in the butter until it's uniformly distributed: using a food processor and the "pulse" function works well. Add zest to the eggs and mix with the flour-butter-sugar mixture until just combined. The dough should be soft, pliable, and not terribly sticky. If it's too crumbly, add a teaspoon of water at a time; if sticky, add a bit of flour, but don't over-work the dough. As with pie crusts, the less you work the dough, the more tender your crust will be. Divide into two uneven pieces (approximately ⅓ and ⅔ each), pat into flat disks, wrap in plastic wrap and refrigerate for 20-30 minutes.

Assembly: Pre-heat the oven to 350 degrees Fahrenheit. Thoroughly grease a 9 inch pie-plate (glass is best). Press the larger piece of dough into the bottom of the dish of the dish and work a ¼ inch lip up around the sides. Spread the jam in a generous, even layer across the dough.

Roll the remaining portion of the dough to ⅛th inch thick, and cut into strips. Place the strips in a cross-hatch pattern across the top and around the edge of the crostata. Finish off the crust by sealing the strips to the edge of the crust by crimping with a fork or your fingers. Bake the crostata for 30-40 minutes or until the crust is golden and the jam begins to bubble. Cool to room temperature before serving.

Crostate can be filled with just about anything: custard, fruit, ricotta, but the "Crostata di Marmellata" is the most basic form. Any good quality jam – or mixture of jams – can be used, but the amount used should be tailored to the quality and intensity of its flavor. A cup of the average, intensely sweet jams found in most supermarkets will create a cloying pastry. Typical jams used in Italy are plum, amarena (sour cherry), and apricot.

Zuppa Inglese

[DZOOP.pah een.GLEH.zeh] ❖ English Soup

Ingredients

2 tsp lemon zest
2 oz semi-sweet baking chocolate
7-17 oz ladyfinger cookies
2 Tbsp dark rum
2 Tbsp Cognac
4 Tbsp dark cherry juice
Dash of bitters (optional)

Crema Pasticcera:
4 egg yolks
¾ c. sugar
1 tsp vanilla
¼ c. flour
2 c. milk

Directions:

Melt the chocolate in a microwave or over a double boiler: set aside. Prepare the Crema Pasticcera and divide into two portions, roughly ⅓ and ⅔. Add the lemon zest to the larger portion and the melted chocolate to the smaller.

Choose a serving dish in which to assemble the *Zuppa*: a 2-quart glass casserole dish or 8 by 8 Pyrex baking dish (or similar) works nicely. Ideally, you want a glass dish, something that is clear and can display the layers.

In a shallow bowl, mix together the liqueurs and cherry juice. Quickly dunk the ladyfingers in this mixture and layer the bottom of your dish, working quickly so that the cookies do not get soggy. Spread about ½ of the lemon-flavored *crema* in a generous layer over the cookies. Layer again with dunked ladyfingers, followed by a layer of the chocolate crema. Place one more layer of dunked ladyfingers, and finish the Zuppa with the remaining lemon crema. Refrigerate for 1 to 2 hours: serve within 6 (this dish doesn't keep well as the ladyfingers get soggy from the liquor and custard over time). Before serving, sift together confectioner's sugar and unsweetened cocoa powder over the crema.

Zuppa Inglese literally translates as "English Soup," a seemingly non-sensical name for this custard-based dessert. Here, "Zuppa" derives from the Italian word "inzuppare", meaning "to dunk", and in fact to make this dish cookies are dunked in Alchermes, a brilliantly red, aromatic liquor. According to one theory "Inglese" originates from efforts to re-create the delicious "English Trifle" that Italian nobles allegedly enjoyed when traveling to England, a major trading partner, in the 16th and 17th centuries.

A Note on Ingredients

This is one of the classic, home-made desserts you might be served if invited over for *pranzo* (lunch) or *cena* (dinner) in many parts of Italy: more refined than a simple *crostata*, but not as complicated (or expensive) as *tiramisu*. It's often topped with dusted cocoa powder, shaved chocolate, and/or whipped cream and served cold.

Alchermes, a slightly bitter, brilliant red aromatic liqueur, is almost impossible to find outside Italy. Here we substitute a mixture of liquors and Bing cherry juice. You can eliminate the alcohol and make this with just cherry juice, perhaps with a dash of bitters for more authenticity, and the *zuppa* is delicious either way.

Ladyfingers are often sold in 200 gr package (7 oz). A popular brand available in Italian specialty stores (and online) is called *Pavesini*, which are small, 64 per 7 oz package. "Savoiardi" style ladyfingers are much bigger, 24 per 7 oz package. The number of cookies you use depends on the size of your serving dish and on the amount of crema. Some versions of this recipe use thinly sliced pound or sponge cake, but at La Romita we use ladyfingers for this recipe, specifically the *Pavesini* type.

Basic *Crema Pasticcera* (Pastry Cream*)***

In a heavy bottomed saucepan, beat together the sugar, egg yolks, and vanilla. Add the flour gradually and mix together well. In a microwave, heat the milk until almost boiling. Slowly add the milk to the egg yolk mixture, stirring constantly to avoid lumps. Cook over low heat for 5 to 10 minutes, stirring constantly in the same direction with a wooden spoon, until the crema clings thickly to it. Do not let it come to a boil (an occasional bubble is fine). Remove from the heat. If leaving to cool, cover with plastic wrap directly touching the cream to prevent a skin from forming.

Tiramisu made by Egizia and Franca

A Camilla
con affetto
Egizia Bonti

A CAMILLA
CON SIMPATIA.

Tiramisu

[tee.rah.mee.SOO]

Ingredients

2 c. espresso coffee
6-8 Tbsp dark rum (optional)
6 egg yolks
⅔ c. sugar
1 ½ lbs mascarpone cheese (chilled)

¾ c. heavy cream (chilled)
¼ tsp salt
14 oz crisp ladyfingers (Savoiardi or similar)
4 Tbsp Dutch process cocoa powder
¼ c. semi-sweet chocolate, grated (optional)

Directions

Stir together the espresso coffee and 4 tablespoons of rum in a wide, shallow bowl or baking dish; set aside. In a large bowl, beat the yolks at low speed with a handheld mixer or in a mixer with a whisk attachment, until just combined. Add the sugar and salt and beat at medium-high speed until pale yellow, 1½ to 2 minutes. Add the remaining rum and beat until just combined, 20-30 seconds. Add the mascarpone cheese and mix together until no lumps remain, 30-45 seconds. Make sure to scrape the bowl between these additions to ensure all ingredients are incorporated. Refrigerate. (For a less alcoholic Tiramisu, reduce or eliminate the rum incorporated into the mascarpone.)

Wash the mixing blades. In a separate bowl, beat the whip cream until stiff peaks form, approximately 3 minutes. Using a spatula, gently fold the whip cream into the mascarpone mixture until no white streaks remain. Refrigerate.

Working one at a time, roll each ladyfinger in the coffee-rum mixture to completely coat (1-2 seconds), remove, and transfer to a 9 by 13 inch glass or ceramic baking dish. Arrange the dipped cookies in a single layer, breaking or trimming ladyfingers as needed to fit neatly. Spread ½ of the mascarpone mixture in a thick layer over the ladyfingers. Sift 2 Tbsp of cocoa power over the mascarpone. Repeat for one additional layer (ladyfingers, mascarpone, cocoa-powder. Cover and refrigerate for at least 4 hours, and up to 24. Garnish with the grated chocolate and serve!

> *The key to this recipe lies in having a fluffy mascarpone layer that contrasts with a cookie layer that is moist, but not soggy. You must use hard ladyfinger cookies, often known as "Savoiardi" – look for ones that are about 4 inches long and ½ inch thick. Quickly roll each cookie in the coffee-rum mixture before placing it in the dish, no more than 2 seconds per cookie.*

Torta Alla Frutta

[TOHR.tah ahl.lah FROO.tah] ❖ Cake with Fruit

Ingredients

Pan di Spagna:
- 3 egg yolks
- 4 egg whites, stiffly beaten
- ¾ c. sugar
- ¾ c. potato starch or corn starch
- 1 c. minus 2 Tbsp all purpose flour
- 1 tsp baking powder
- 1 tsp vanilla
- ½ tsp salt
- 6 Tbsp water

Filling:
- 2 ½ c. crema pasticcera (p. 79)
- 1 c. crushed pineapple in syrup
- ½ c. (approx.) rum or *Prosecco*
- 1 ½ c. heavy cream
- 3 Tbsp sugar (extra fine is best)

Directions

For the Pan di Spagna ("Spanish Cake"- a basic sponge cake): Preheat an oven to 350 degrees Farenheit. Prepare a 9 by 13 inch baking pan or two 9-inch cake rounds by buttering generously and lining the bottoms with parchment paper. In a large mixing bowl, beat together the egg yolks, sugar, vanilla and water. In a separate bowl, mix together the flour, salt, starch and baking powder. Add this to the egg mixture, stirring just enough to incorporate all ingredients. Gently fold in the beaten egg whites one third at time, being careful not to overmix. Pour the batter into the prepared pan(s), level with a spatula, and bake for 25 -30 minutes or until a toothpick inserted in the center comes out dry. Cool for a few minutes, then run a knife around the edges of the pan to loosen. Invert the cake(s) onto a wire rack or unfolded brown paper bag to finish cooling.

This layer cake is full everything that makes Italian desserts from this region so delightful- fruit, custard, whipped cream, and a splash of rum or Prosecco (a dry Italian sparkling wine made in the Champagne style and most often served as an aperitif). Torta di Frutta is Egizia's favorite dessert for special occasions, birthdays, and holidays. You can divide the cake batter between two 9-inch cake rounds, or make one 9 by 13 sheet cake and cut it into halves or thirds.

For the Fillings:

Prepare the Crema Pasticcera according to the instructions for Zuppa Inglese (pg 70), adjusting the proportions as follows: 2 c. milk, 2 eggs, ¼ c. sugar, 3 Tbsp flour, and a bit of lemon rind. This will yield approximately 2½ cups of custard: Cool to room temperature. Drain the pineapple and reserve the syrup. Whip together the 1½ c. heavy cream and 3 Tbsp sugar to make whipped cream.

Assembly: Lay one sponge cake round (or ½ of the sheet cake) on a suitable serving dish. Brush with ¼ c. of the reserved pineapple syrup and, if desired, ¼ rum or Prosecco. Top with half of the crushed pineapple and a generous layer of the crema pasticcera. Place the second cake on top and repeat. Chill for 15-20 minutes in the refrigerator or freezer.

Using a spatula or pastry bag, cover the entire cake with the whipped cream, garnishing the top if desired with additional fresh or preserved fruit, sprinkles or pieces of shaved chocolate. This cake is best eaten slightly chilled.

Assisi – Charlotte Britton

Limoncello

[lee.mohn.CHEL.loh]

Ingredients

10 lemons (Meyer or organic)
1 Liter (4 ¼ cups) 151 proof (75%) flavorless
    grain alcohol (such as Everclear)
4 c. sugar

4 ¼ c. filtered water
A large glass jar (non-reactive) to store the liquor
Additional glass bottles, with stoppers, for the
    finished limoncello

Directions

There are 3 keys to preparing good limoncello: (1) quality -- select high-quality lemons with a lot of flavor, (2) care -- zest them carefully, using only the yellow peel, and (3) patience – the lemons must macerate for 30-40 days.
Wash the lemons thoroughly with a sponge or produce brush. Carefully remove the yellow outer rind of the lemons using either a microplane grater or a lemon zester. Inclusion of the bitter, white pith will result in a bitter limoncello. The smaller the lemon peel flakes, the greater the chance for the essential lemon oils to dissolve in the alcohol.

Mix the lemon zest and alcohol together in a large non-reactive container (glass jar) and wait for at least 30 days, stirring the mixture every 5 to 7 days. Keep this mixture in a cool, dry place (refrigerator or a cool basement) while it steeps. At the end of 30 -40 days, the alcohol will have taken on a distinct yellow color, showing the lemon oils have left the zest, which will be pale and brittle. Strain the alcohol from the zest with a very fine sieve—a coffee filter can work--and discard the zest.

In a large saucepan, combine the sugar and water and cook over medium-high heat just until the sugar dissolves. Do not allow mixture to boil. Remove from heat and cool to room temperature. Combine the alcohol and sugar solution and mix thoroughly. The limoncello is done! It can be enjoyed immediately, but its flavor will continue to develop as it ages and will be better after an additional 4 to 6 weeks, during which time it can be stored in the freezer. Serve chilled (like Vodka), in tall shot glasses.

This sweet after-dinner liqueur, now common throughout Italy, originated in the early 1900s on the Amalfi coast, on or near the island of Capri, although the nearby communities of Amalfi and Sorrento (still famous for its lemon groves) also claim to be its inventors. In Italy it's still common for families to manufacture their own after-dinner liquers or amari (digestive bitters) using recipes passed down through generations.

Caffé

A cappuccino in the morning on the way to work, *un caffè* when meeting a friend at *Il Bar,* shared over the dining table when visiting a friend, or to mark the end of a meal. Coffee is as crucial and as inseparable from life in Italy as pasta. And while espresso-based drinks in the U.S. have become a common punchline ("I'll have a triple grande whipped half-caff iced latte with caramel"), Italy has but a small core of variations found in every bar or restaurant that boasts an espresso machine.

Caffè - When in Italy you don't ask for an espresso, you ask for *un caffè* - "a coffee". *Un caffè* is around an ounce of extremely strong coffee, topped with a caramel-colored foam called *crema*, which is formed by the action of the high-pressure restaurant-quality espresso machines. Most Italians sweeten their *caffè* with one or more teaspoons of sugar, drink it in one or two sips, and use a spoon to scoop up the delicious *crema*.

Cappuccino - the quintessential morning coffee: a shot of espresso topped topped with a thick head of foamed milk: the ratio of coffee to milk is about 1:1. Italians do not usually drink cappuccino after 11AM!

Caffè macchiato - *Macchiato* means "colored" or "stained", in this case, a shot of espresso is colored by a little steamed milk, perhaps garnished with a touch of foam. This is served in the same demitasse cup (*tazzina*) as an espresso. You can also order "latte macchiato", which is milk "stained" with a little coffee.

Caffè e latte - espresso with more steamed milk, closer to a 1:2 ratio of coffee to milk, with less foam. When in Italy, remember to order this drink by its full name "*caffè e latte*". Merely ordering a *latte* will get you a glass of steamed milk!

Caffè corretto – "Correct" coffee with a drizzle of liquor, particularly common north of Bologna: generally grappa, but sambucca, cognac, and rum are common choices.

ABOUT THE AUTHORS

Amina and Alessandro are the children of Paola Quargnali, the sister of La Romita School co-founder Enza Quargnali. Paola became involved in La Romita in the early 1970s: a university lecturer and later high-school teacher she helped define La Romita School's mission of encouraging cross-cultural educational exchange. Paola shared her passion for Italy's culture and beauty with her children who, along with Enza's son Lars, are involved in carrying forward the La Romita School mission into the next generation. Alessandro lives in Chicago where he splits time between La Romita and a career as a Systems Administrator. Food is a passion he shares with his wife, Joanna, and which he is working to impart to his young daughter in bite size pieces. Amina, an attorney, is a Judge Advocate in the Air Force Reserve. She lives with her husband, Dave, and their two children in Bangkok, Thailand, where he is assigned as a defense attaché to the United States Embassy

To find out more about La Romita, see our current list of workshops, sign on to our newsletter, or just say *ciao*, visit, write, or call:

Website: www.laromita.org
Email: schoolinfo@laromita.org
Facebook: www.facebook.com\laromitaschool

Address: La Romita School of Art
          P.O. Box 58219
          Washington, DC 20037

Tel: 1-855-4ROMITA

Made in the USA
Lexington, KY
22 September 2018